FOX
COLORING BOOK
BELONGE TO

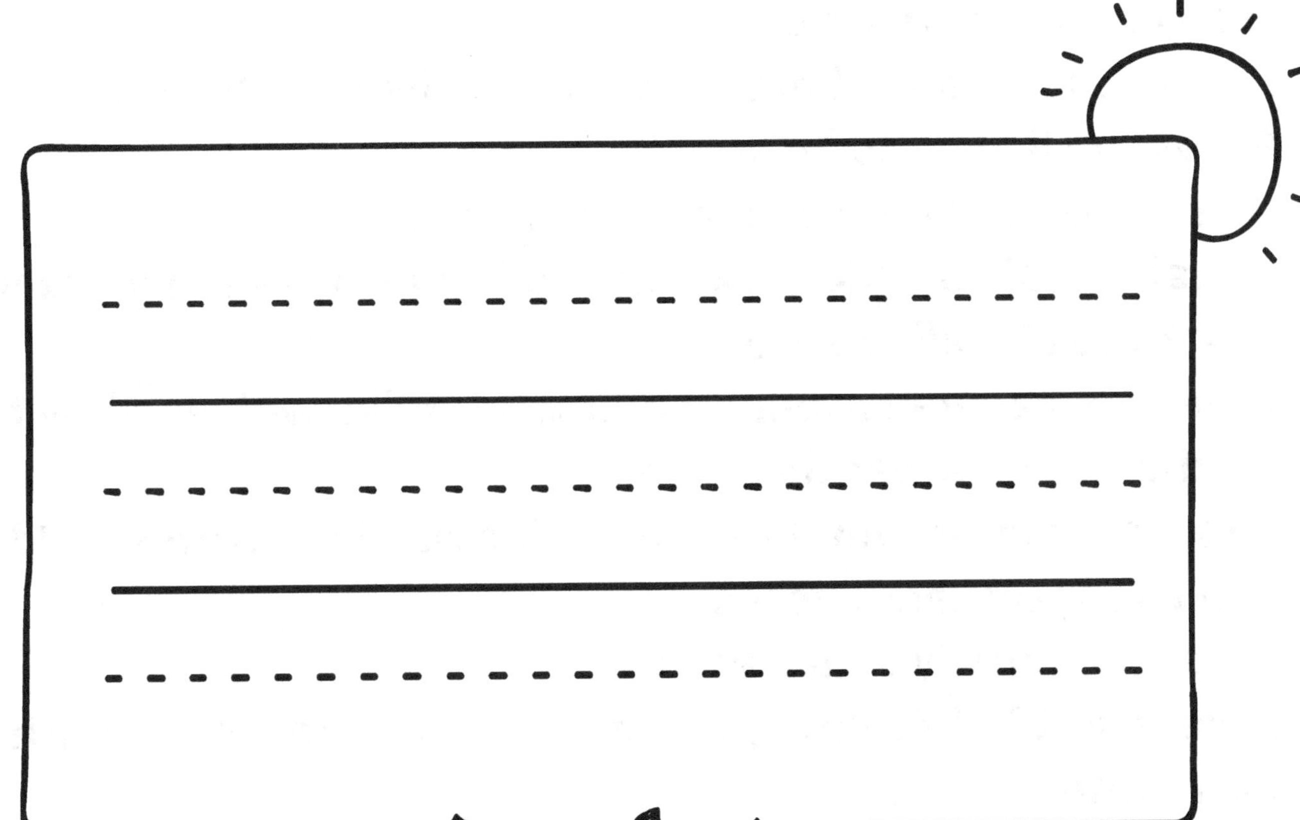

<u>Some Fascinating Facts About Foxes</u>

- Foxes are one of the most well known wild animals in the UK, they are native to Britain.
- Foxes can live anywhere, in towns or the countryside
- Foxes can live up to 14 years
- A group of foxes is called a skulk or leash
- A male is called a 'dog fox' while a female is called a 'vixen'
- A baby fox is called a cub
- Foxes are generally solitary animals; unlike wolves, they hunt on their own rather than in packs
- Foxes eat almost anything, including berries, worms, spiders and even jam sandwiches
- Foxes are mostly active at night
- Foxes use 28 different types of calls to communicate with each other
- A fox can run 30 miles per hour
- The Smallest FOX weight under 3 pounds.
- ARCTIC FOXES DON'T SHIVER UNTIL -70° CELSIUS.
- The latin name for fox is "Vulpes Vulpes"
- Foxes are mostly active at night
- Foxes hide food to eat later
- Foxes dig underground dens where they take care of their kits and hide from predators

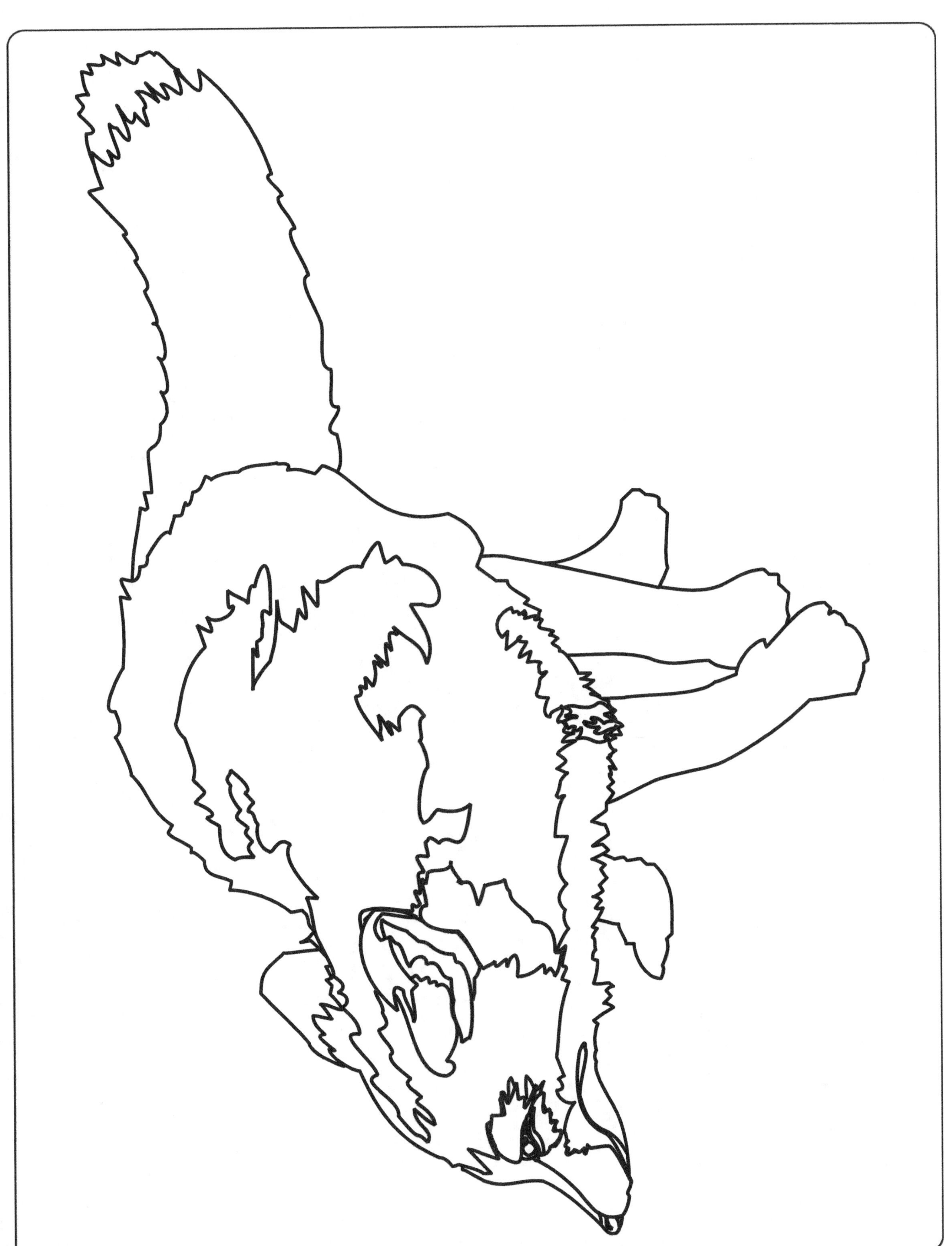

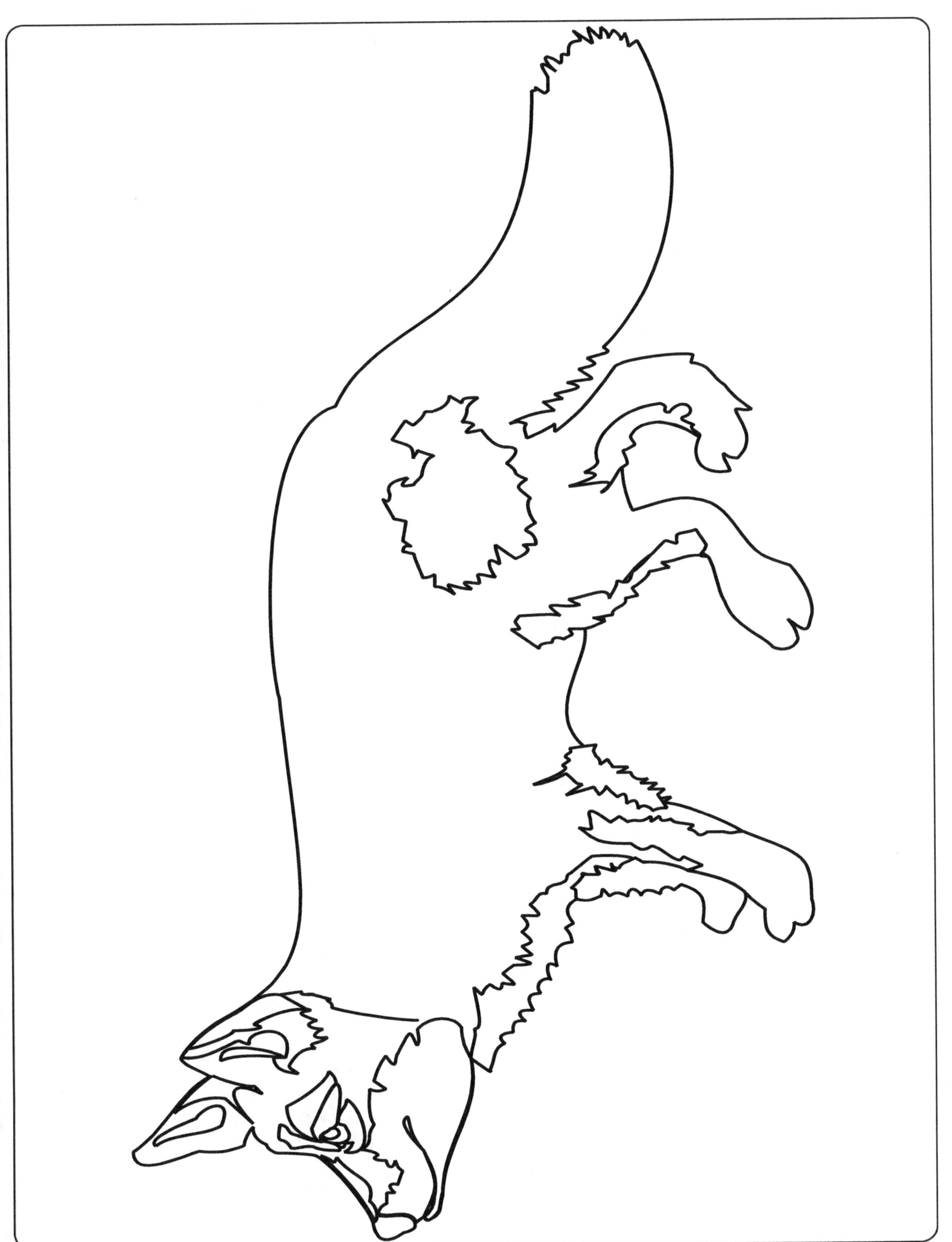

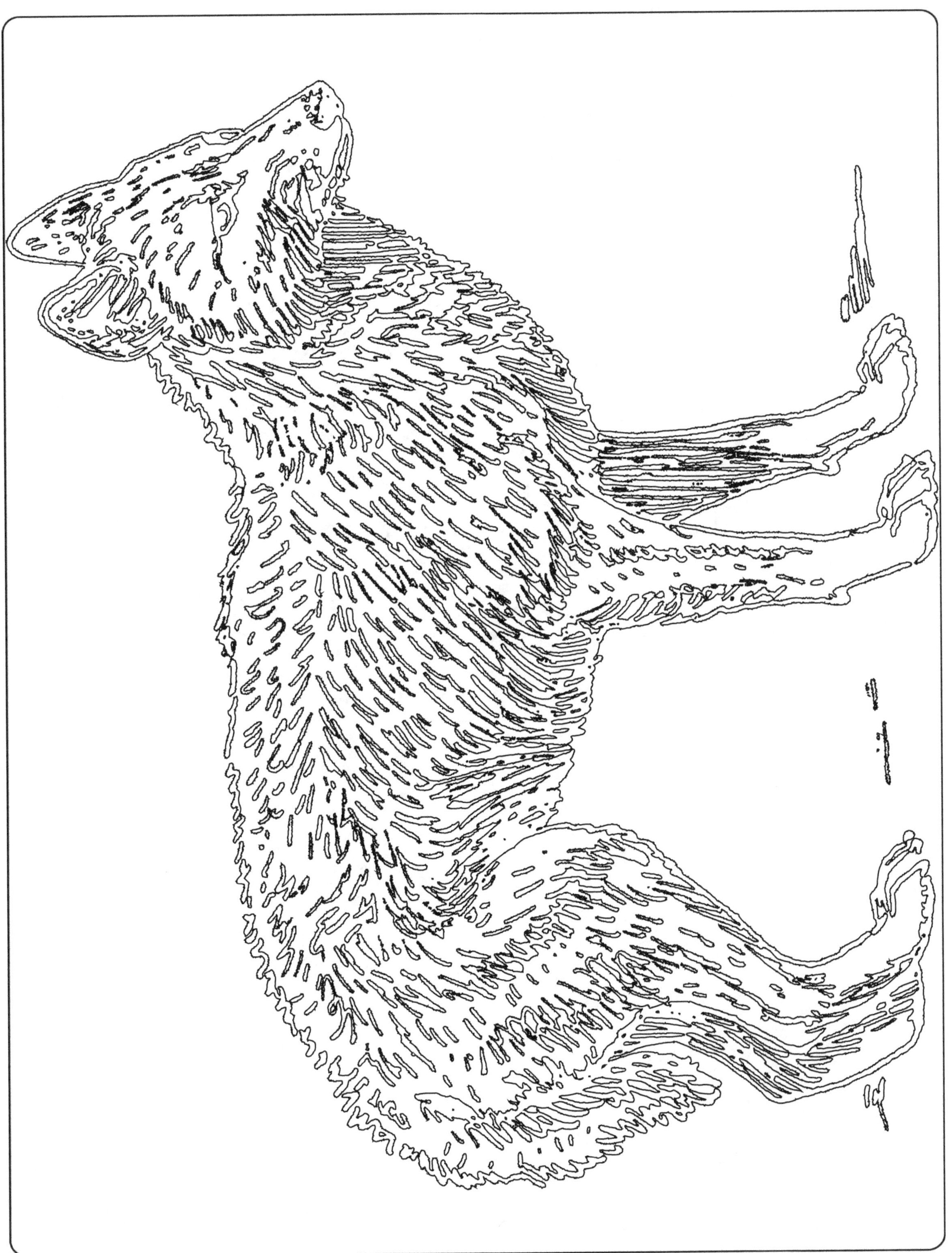

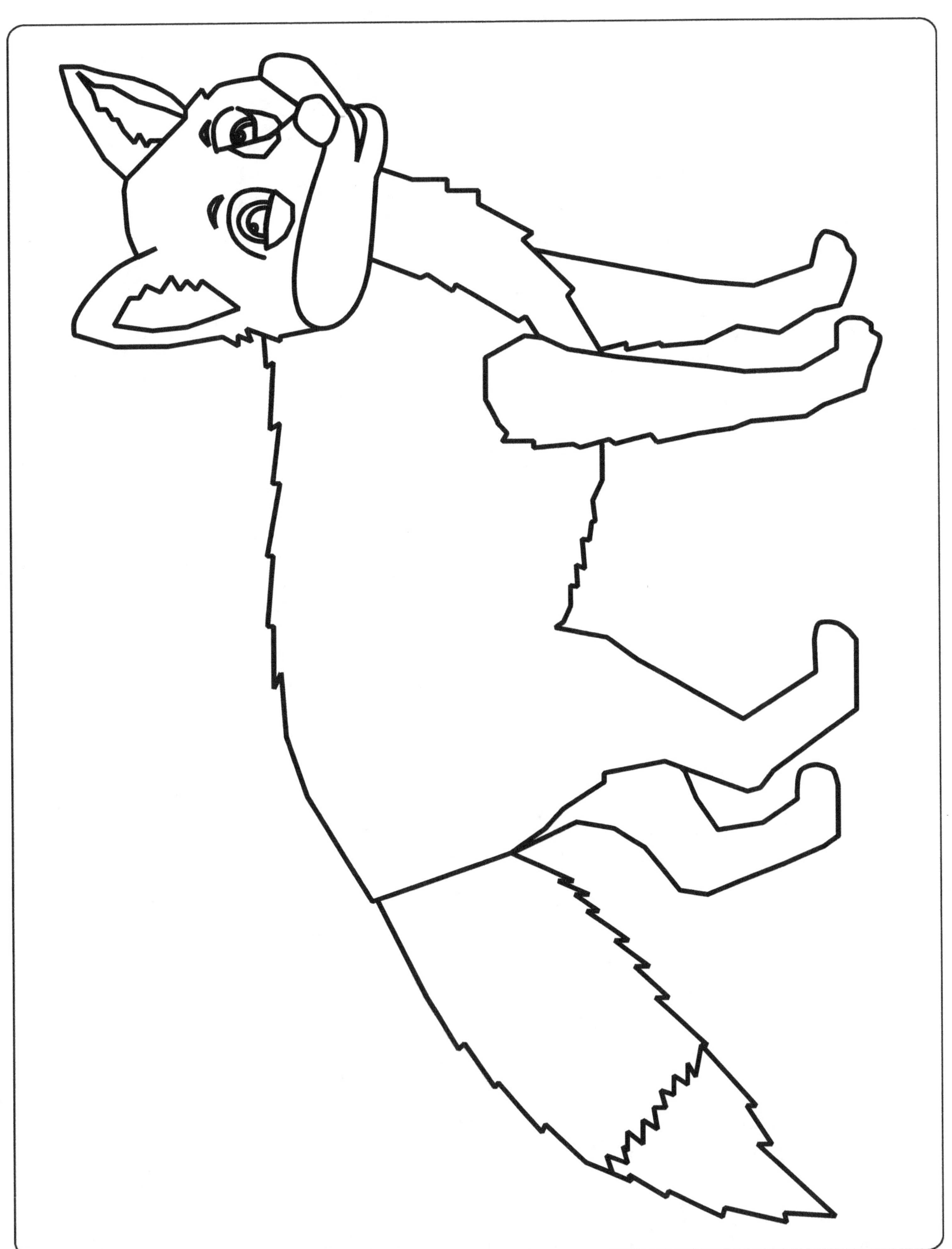

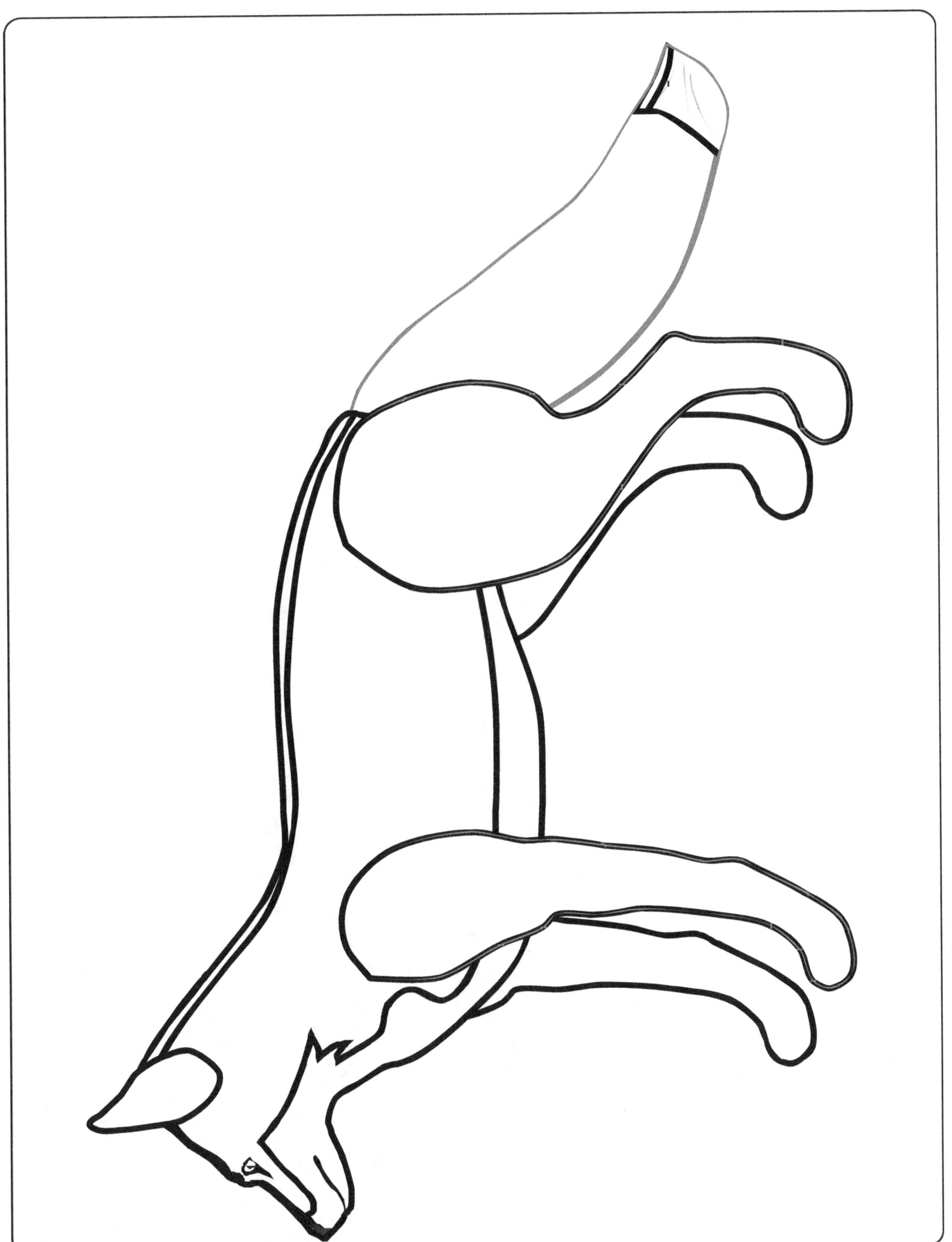

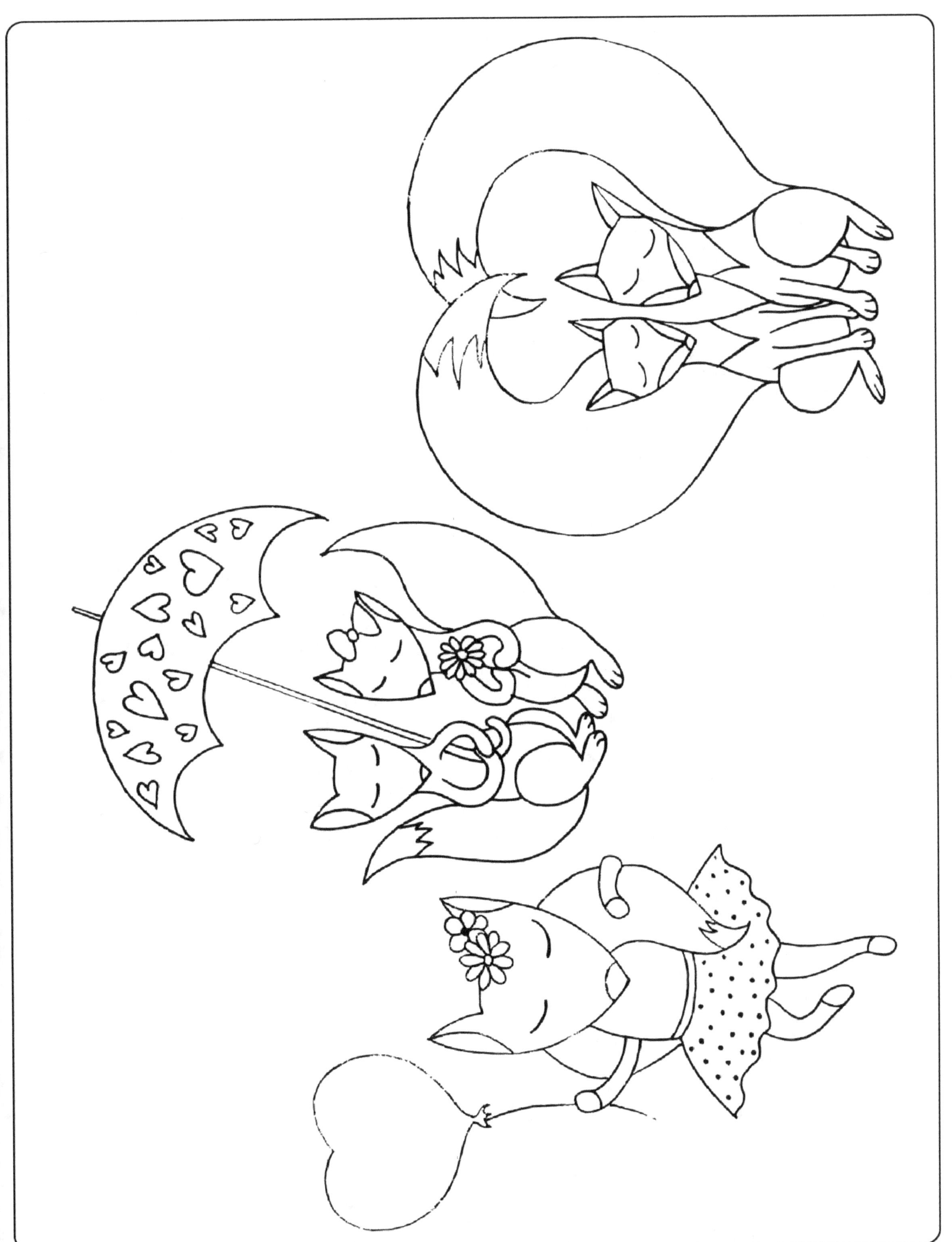

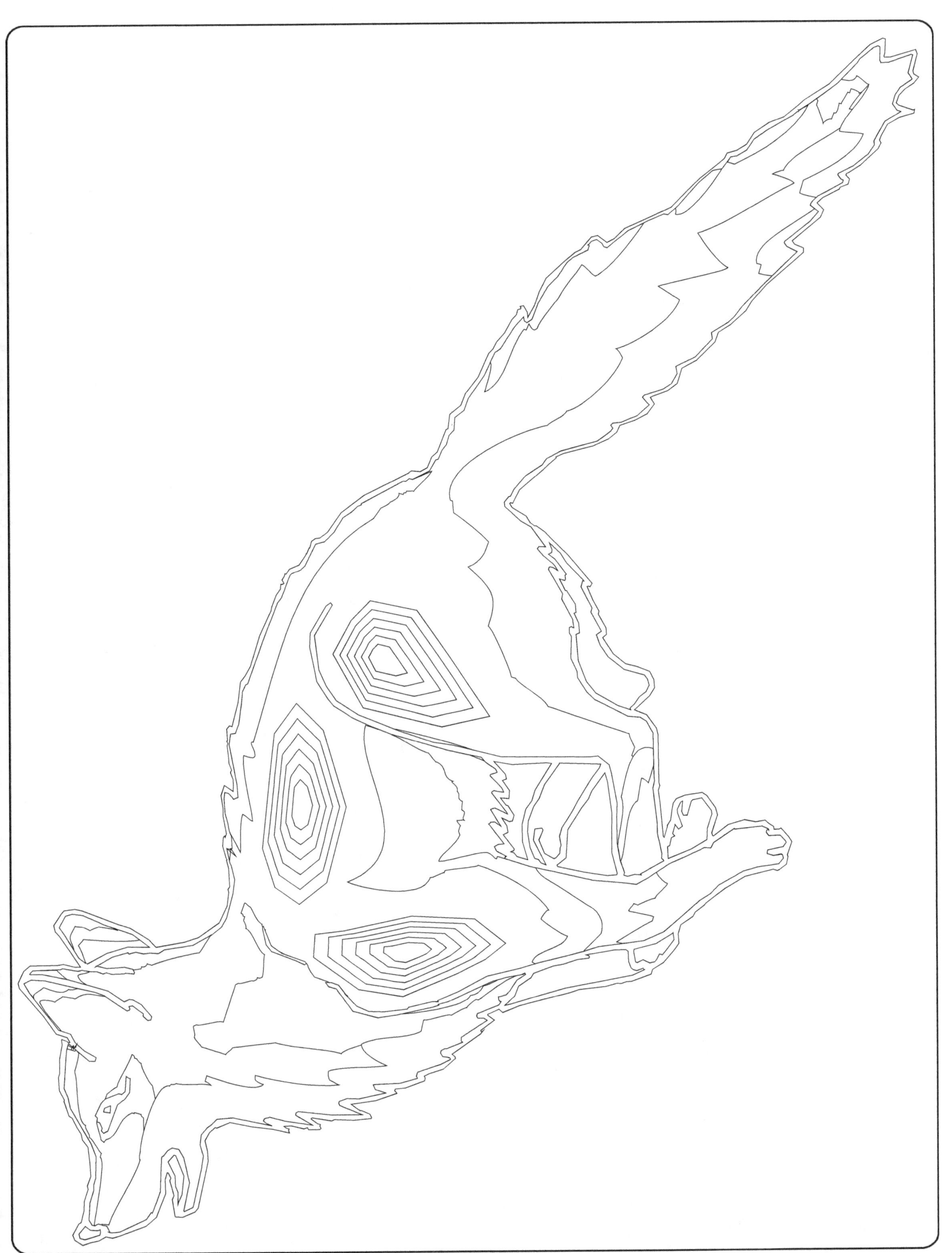

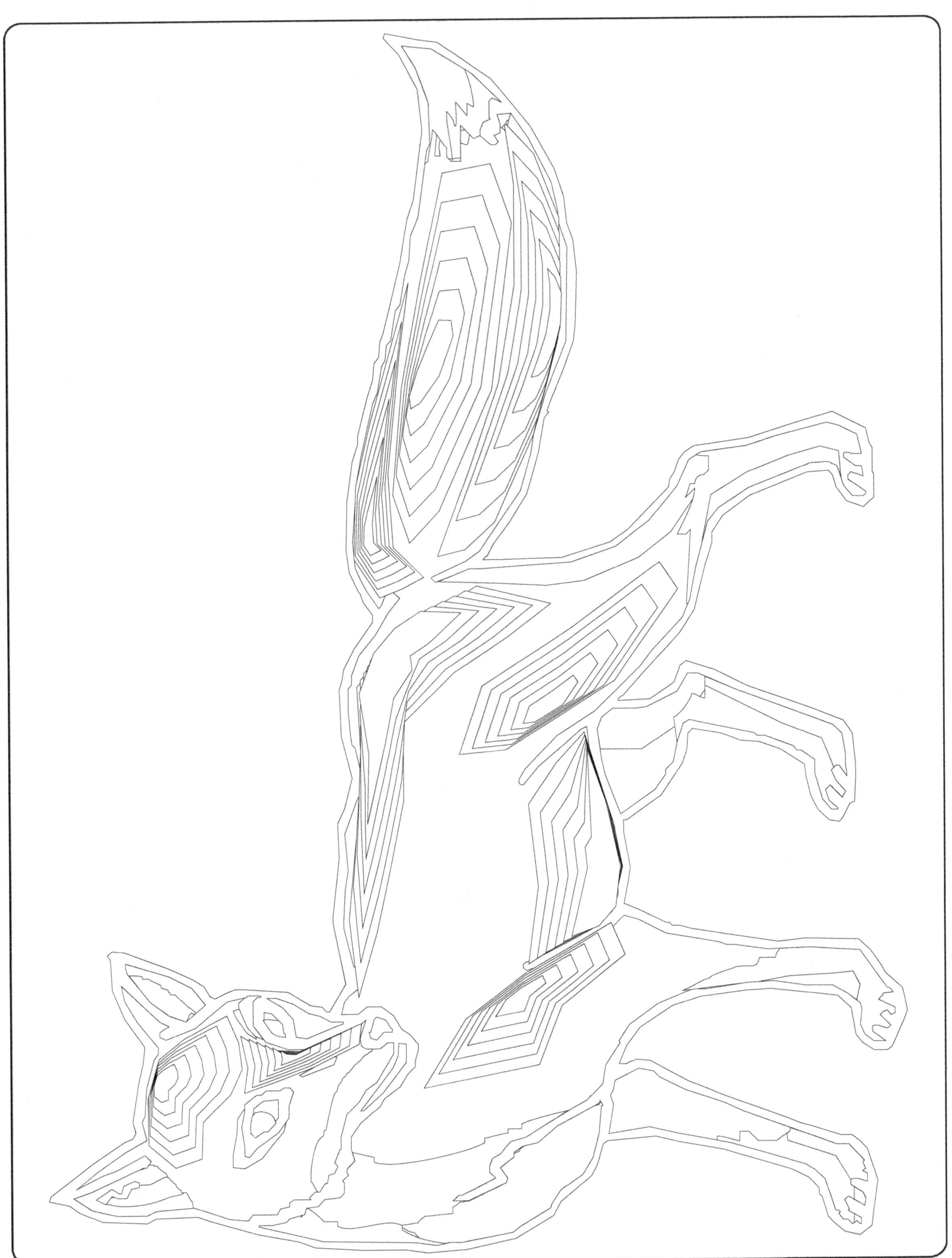

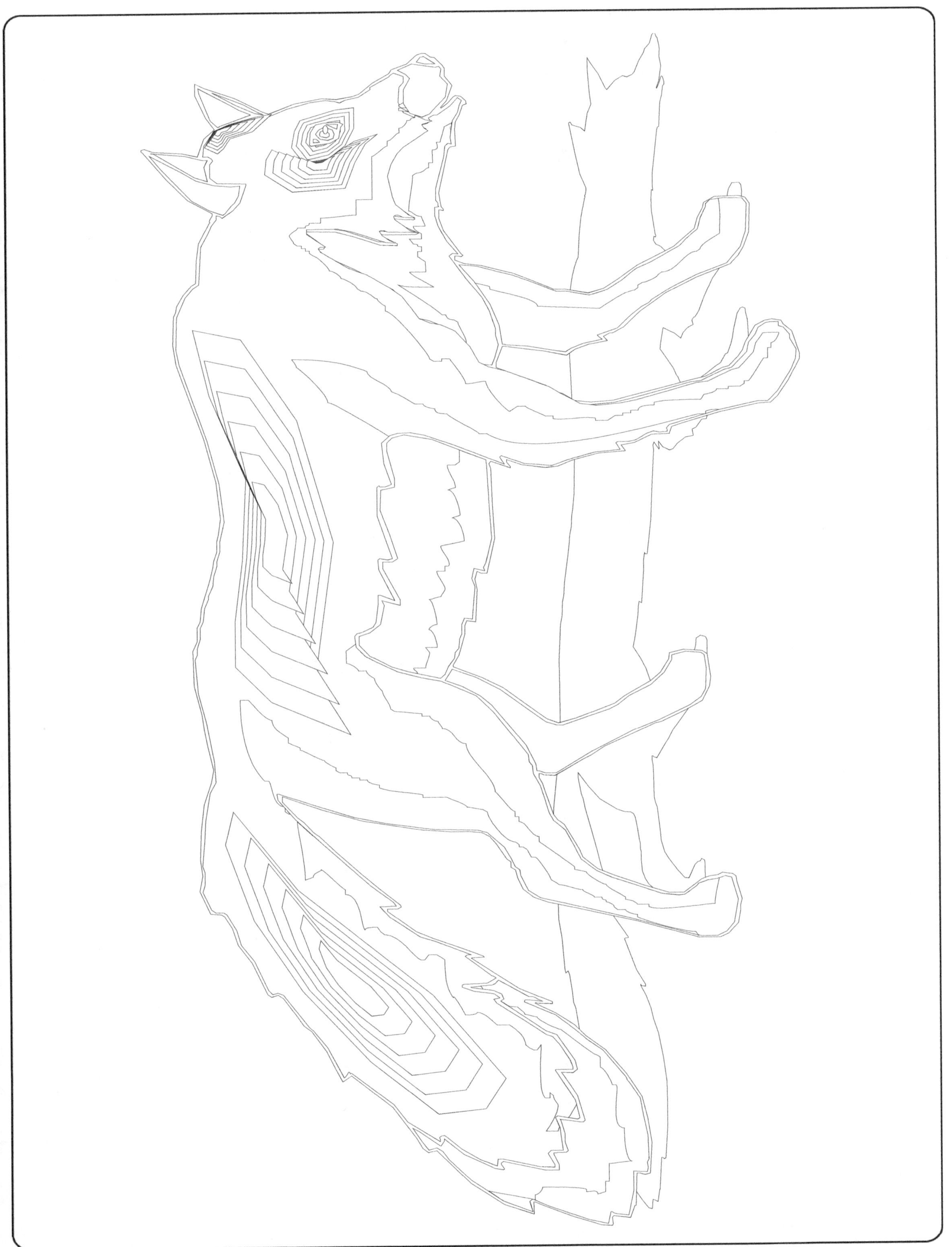

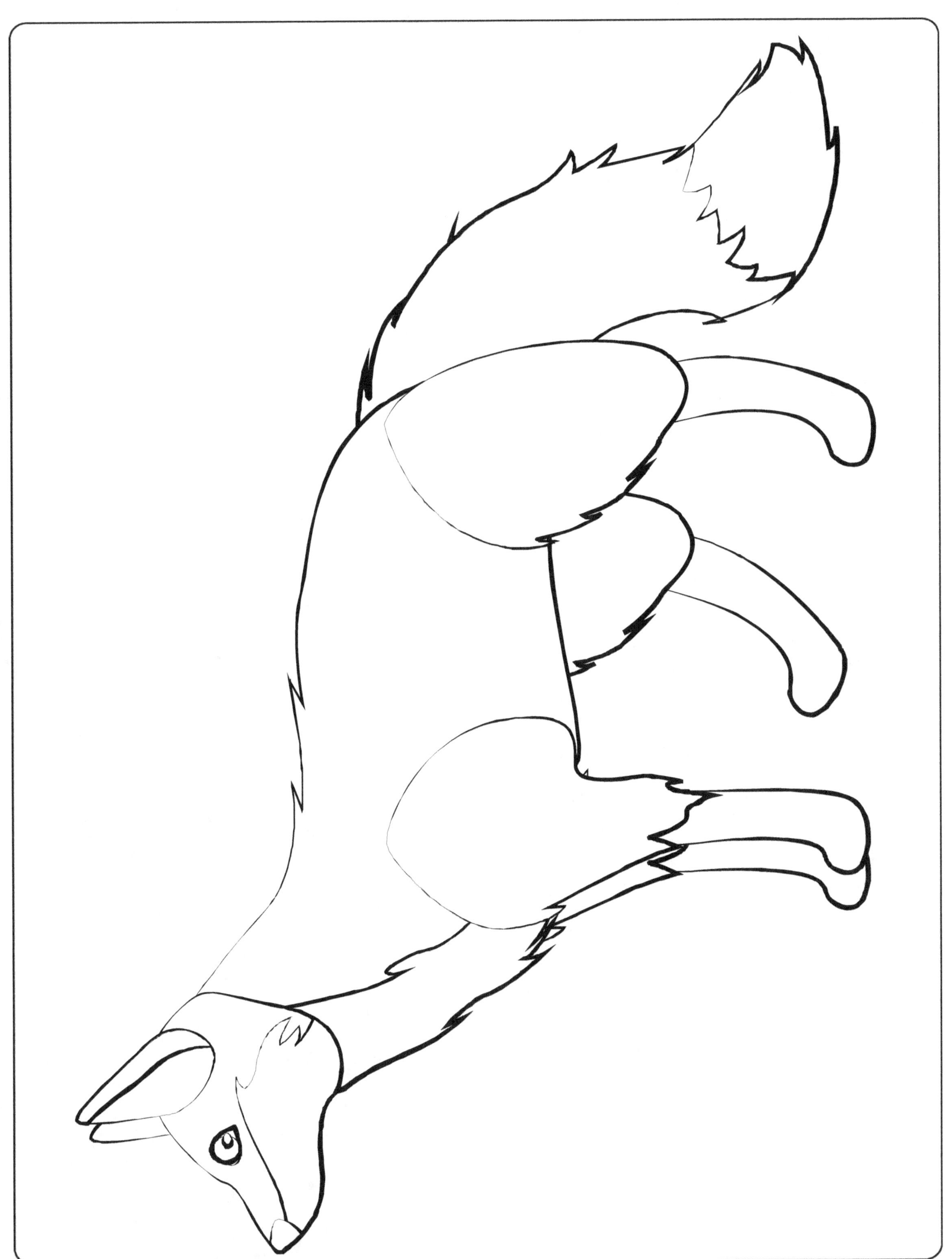

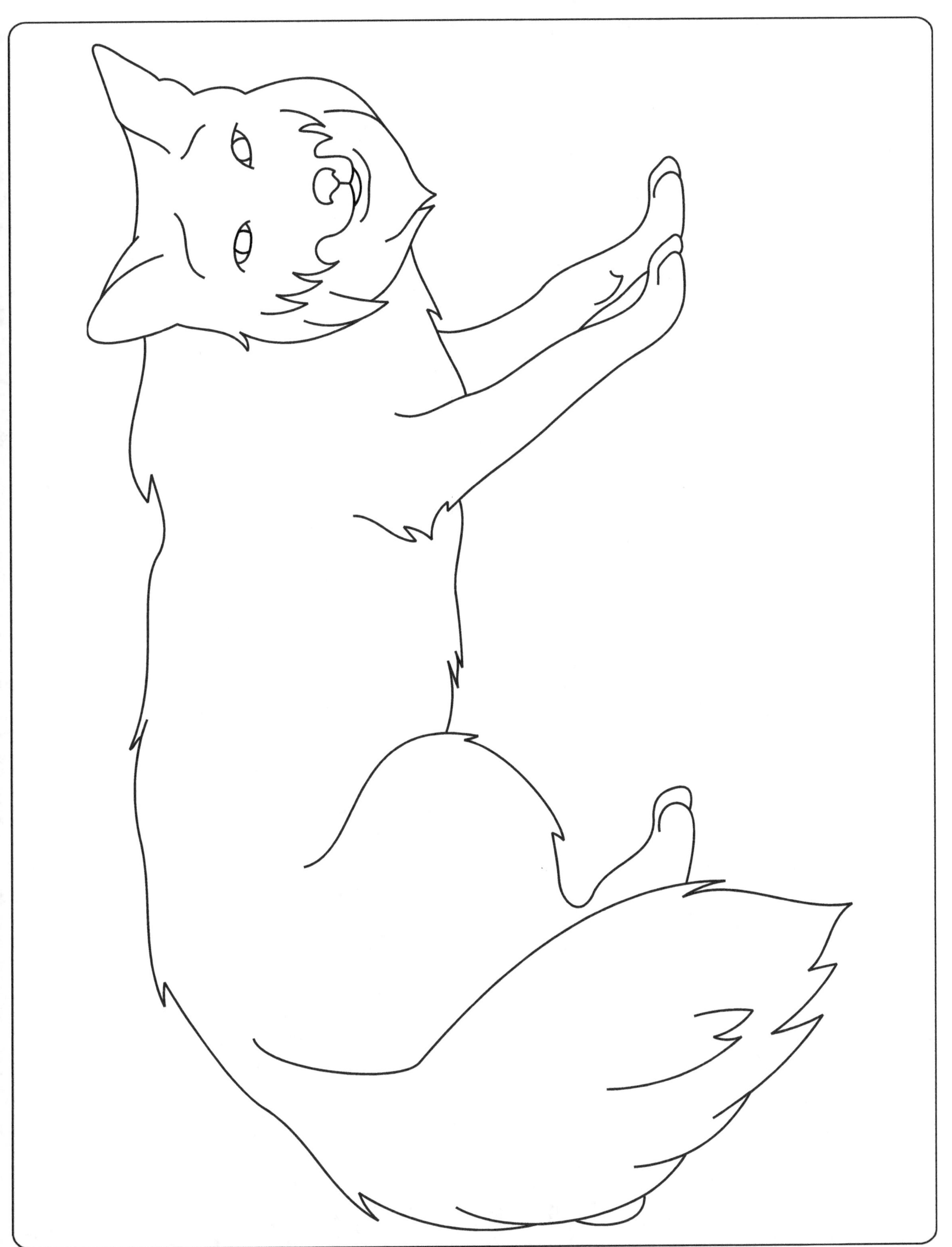

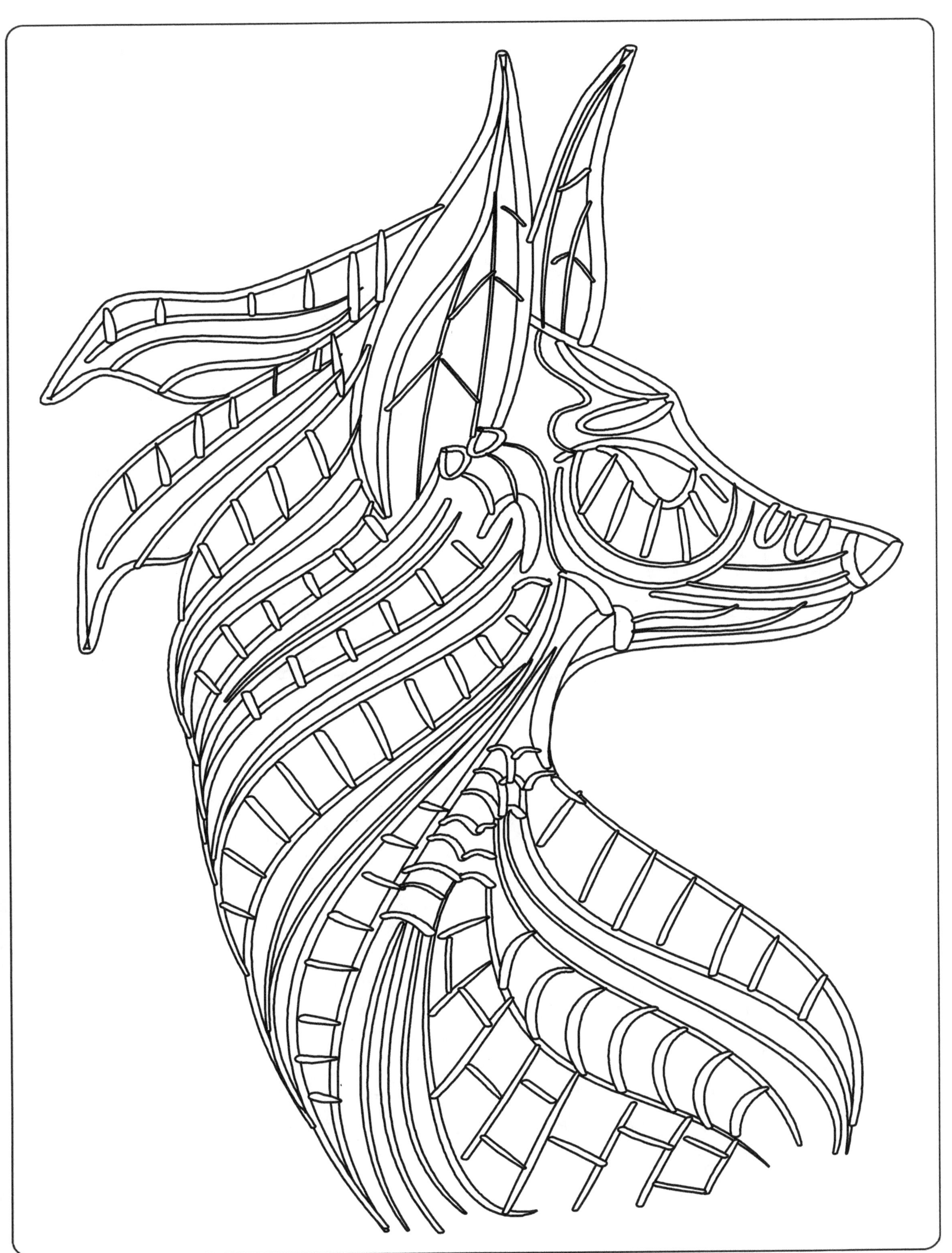

COLOR TEST PAGE

COLOR TEST PAGE

www.ingramcontent.com/pod-product-compliance
Lightning Source LLC
Chambersburg PA
CBHW081307250726
48662CB00008B/2439